World of
CATS

TO PAINT OR COLOR

John Green

Dover Publications, Inc.
Mineola, New York

Note

Cats are curious, adorable, and have a keen zest for life. People enjoy watching their antics as they explore, hunt, and play. Nowadays, cats have become the most popular household pet—even bypassing dogs! Here we have assembled twenty-three illustrations for you to color featuring some fabulous felines including an elegant, longhaired cat posing on a pillow, rambunctious kittens playing with yarn, and a young girl hugging her favorite furry friend.

Watch the printed lines practically disappear as you create your own personal masterpieces using pencil, pen, paint or any other media. The illustrations are printed on one side only on high-quality paper making them suitable for framing when completed. To remove the pages, carefully tear them out following the perforation.

Copyright

Copyright © 2007 by Dover Publications, Inc.
All rights reserved.

Bibliographical Note

World of Cats to Paint or Color is a new work, first published by Dover Publications, Inc., in 2007.

International Standard Book Number
ISBN-13: 978-0-486-46233-2
ISBN-10: 0-486-46233-1

Manufactured in the United States by Courier Corporation
46233103   2013
www.doverpublications.com